MW01113688

Unsung Heroes, Villains, Victims, and Guides

Original Stories from Bakersfield Writers Volume One

Kathryn Buys, Carla Joy Martin, Ryan Vaughn, Kevin Shah, Scott Brown

SHAH & BROWN WRITING WORKSHOPS
RIVERBLUFF RANCH 2021

Our Cover Photo - Gordon's Ferry – 144 Years before our Writers' Conference on the Banks of the Kern River

---------------------------- o ----------------------------

According to Wikipedia, Gordon's Ferry "is both a geographical location and a historic site in Bakersfield, California. It is located close to where China Grade Loop crosses the Kern River and meets with Alfred Harrell Highway in Northeast Bakersfield. It is name after a ferry that used to cross the river near the existing bridge. It was one of the only eastern crossings, until 1877, when the Jewett Avenue bridge was constructed farther west. It is California Historical Landmark #137."

The River – An Introduction

This compendium publication represents the work of five of the many writers who attended a 4-week writing workshop with newer, experienced, and advanced writers in Bakersfield, California. The stories explore the heroes, villains, victims, and guides in our lives. I am grateful to memoirist Donald Miller for explaining that these are four main character archetypes in literature.

We met four Saturday mornings on the banks of the Kern River at Riverbluff Ranch owned by Terry Delamater. No Zoom sessions, no stuffy buildings, just nature and us. With the "wings" of proven brainstorming techniques, we took to the sky of writing like the Canada geese that took flight from the flowing river beside us. The burbling of the river seemed to say, "Flow, just flow." And the river seemed to hear us as well, echoing what inspiration we'd found in our guided brainstorming.

Why this resonance? I imagine we were one with the river because we are composed mostly of water – with a few inner trees, hills, bees, and seasonal flowers. We plan on making *Unsung Heroes, Villains, Victims and Guides* as a series. The writing workshops represent our desire to bring many years of writing and independent publishing guidance to local writers - Kevin Shah & Scott Brown

Our Brand Promise

We use the power of human connection to produce creative communities for writers to grow in the craft and achieve their publishing goals by using products and services that gently guide and are as unique as the individuals we serve.

SHAH & BROWN Unlimited Copyright Page

This is a compendium of authors' work
offering both fact and fiction.
The events and characters described herein
are both real and imaginary
and may refer to specific places or living persons
as noted for each story.
The opinions expressed in this manuscript are solely
the opinions of the authors and do not represent the opinions or
thoughts of the publisher.
The authors have represented and warranted full
ownership and/or legal right to publish all the
materials in this book.

Unsung Heroes, Villains, Victims and Guides

All Rights Reserved.
Version 1.0 Copyright © 2021, **ISBN: 978-1-7377557-0-8**
Kathryn Buys, Carla Joy Martin, Ryan Vaughn,
Kevin Shah, Scott Brown

This book may not be reproduced, transmitted, or stored in
whole or in part by any means, including graphic, electronic, or
mechanical without the express written consent of the publisher
except in the case of brief quotations embodied in critical
articles and reviews.

SHAH & BROWN Unlimited, Nova Publishing Division
Bakersfield, California
Nova Publishing and the "*NOVA*" logo are service marks
belonging to Nova Publishing
Bakersfield, California

Unsung Heroes, Villains, Victims and Guides

Original Stories from Bakersfield Writers

Table of Contents

Chocolate-Covered Sticky Buns

by Carla Joy Martin

I remember what happened to me one "misty moisty morning" (as the nursery rhyme goes) when I was five years old at First Form School in St. Andrews, Scotland. I was running across the playground with a chocolate-covered sticky bun that my friend, Lucy Abercrombie, and I had just purchased from the lorry that came to the school every day. In my excitement over having such a treasure, I tripped and dropped the donut face-down onto the asphalt.

Lucy scooped up the sticky bun and carried it to the drinking fountain and washed it off. "There," she proclaimed, "now it's as good as new!"

I felt such a relief! I could eat it after all! I can still taste that watery, sweet, doughy donut in my mouth when I recollect this occurrence.

Lucy could always find a way forward. With her curly chestnut hair and upturned nose, she was the picture of curious optimism. When I thought of her, I heard irrepressible laughter.

When I left Scotland to come back to the United States, Lucy gave me a miniature Gaelic cross sitting on a small block of viridian marble. "The green stone comes from the land around St. Andrews, and this is St. Andrew's cross," she told me. I kept this treasure in my padded powder blue jewelry box as a child and would look at it and remember my friend.

Lucy and I became pen pals. I eagerly opened her letters, written in a tiny cursive script with a nibbed pen. In one letter she told me about her skiing escapades that she illustrated with hilarious little stick figures. Another letter described her experiences when she spent a semester at a college in Georgia in the States, studying Southern architecture. Lucy's boundless enthusiasm and sense of humor always came through.

Finally came the day when we could reconnect in person. I traveled back to Scotland after my freshman year in college and wrote to Lucy beforehand, asking if we could spend some time together.

I met her at a bus stop in Edinburgh. She took out two red clown noses out of her bag and said, "Put this on – it'll be fun to see what people do when they see us!"

I was embarrassed and balked at drawing attention to myself. I always wanted to fit in and be perfect. How could I possibly put on a ridiculous rubber nose in front of people I'd never even met?

But Lucy's twinkling eyes encouraged me onward, so I put the clown nose on my face. We got on the bus. People glanced up, then did a double-take, and smiled. Instead of embarrassed, I felt euphoric, like I had slayed a dragon.

After that bus ride, Lucy took me to have dinner with her parents. We all had a homemade lasagna dinner followed by delicious raspberry trifle, and Lucy wrote the recipes out for me in my spiral bound notebook. Then we agreed to meet again in St. Andrews later that summer. I marveled how we managed to just pick right up from where we left off so many years before.

In St. Andrews, Lucy welcomed me to her little student flat and then took me to an artist's studio who made etchings of landmark buildings of the town. I bought some posters. When our visit came to an end, Lucy presented me with a delicate silver thistle on a slender chain. She said, "The thistle is the official flower of Scotland. This will make you an official Scot!" When the necklace wasn't around my neck, I kept it in my now-faded padded powder blue jewelry box, next to Lucy's cross.

After college, Lucy wrote me and said she and her "significant other," Bram, were living in an old barn in Northern Ireland which they had remodeled. It had a thatched roof which was a challenge to replace. It sounded so romantic, I thought. And daring to live with a man and not be married to him – this was beyond my comprehension at the time.

~   ~   ~

The years flew by. I got married, had two boys, divorced, and after fifteen years of being single, found a new boyfriend. Elated, I wanted to share my happiness with others. But I had lost track of Lucy. Our letters had stopped crossing the Atlantic for quite some time. How was my old friend? I decided to look Lucy up.

I searched Facebook but only found her brother listed. Undaunted, I explained my quest to my new boyfriend, and he did some expediting on the Internet. He found an address and I sent a letter off. Several months went by. No response. So my boyfriend searched some more, found the company Lucy was working for as an architect and gave them a call. Did a Lucy Abercrombie still work for them? He explained he was calling for a childhood friend of hers that used to go to school with her in St. Andrews before she moved back to the United States. "This old friend would really like to reconnect with her....do you know how we could reach her?"

The receptionist said Lucy still worked for them and would give her the message. I emailed her the same missive I wrote in the original letter. In the letter, I'm afraid I gushed a bit about my new "soulmate." I also

brought her up to date on how my parents and sons were

doing, then I told her I still had her recipes for lasagna and

trifle. I asked if she was still living with Bram in the

thatched-roof barn. Then I closed with these words: "As

one reflects on one's life in these, the 'Golden Years,' one is

grateful for friends who have been a bit of sunshine on a

cloudy, cold day. You have been such a friend, Lucy. I

hope to hear from you!"

Several days later, I received this email back:

Dear Carla,

I'm glad to hear life is going well for you and your

family and that you've found a soulmate.

My life too is going well, but in another direction to

yours and I'm afraid your tracking me down does sound

like stalking, and is an unwelcome reminder that it's hard to obtain privacy in this day and age.

The last time you imposed yourself, through contact using my work email, got me into trouble with my employers – I politely humored you then but not this time.

I won't be responding any further; I don't share the same desire to renew a distant acquaintance after all these years.

Best wishes and goodbye.

Please don't reply to this.

Lucy

My heart fell into my stomach. I felt like I'd been slapped in the face. Tears welled up. I reread the email again. Incredulous, I whispered, "Is this really Lucy?"

I was stunned. What had happened to the cheerful, daring, warm-hearted girl I remembered? Why wasn't she happy to hear from me? I never got the message in which she "politely humored" me. Did I really get her in trouble with her employers? But they had seemed cheerful and only too eager to help two old friends find each other. What had hurt her and turned her so vindictive? Perhaps Bram left her for another woman and all my news about my new boyfriend just opened up old wounds? Or maybe I was the deluded one – I really was just a "distant acquaintance" that didn't make much of a blip in her radar of memories.

But I still have my cherished memories of Lucy. And I mourn for the girl that once was.

Carla Joy Martin is a poet, pianist and pastel artist residing in Bakersfield, CA. She received a MA in English Literature from Stanford. She is an avid supporter of the arts in her community. Carla published her first poetry chapbook, A Kaleidoscope of Love, in 2020.

The Great Dog Boone in
Sir Kit's Imagination Engine

by Ryan Vaughn

It had been a hard day.

I had been rejected for a writing job I had put a lot of effort into applying for. I knew it had been a long shot but the rejection still stung. This was a compounding event upon others that span too much time to effectively relate here but suffice to say that things had been difficult on all fronts and this seeming final loss felt insurmountable in the moment. After some casual substance abuse, I settled in for a long shower, sitting down in the corner to just let the water hit me as my mind wandered.

In the midst of my wallowing, I thought I heard scratching at the bathroom door. "Rommel?" I called weakly; my housemate might be mad my shower was taking so long. No answer. "Rommel?" A little louder. Still nothing. I closed my eyes and settled back into the corner. A few seconds later more scratches broke the sounds of rushing water, followed by a high-pitched whine. "Rommel?" Concerned this time. Maybe he was just being weird. "I'll be out in a sec." I stood up, frustrated, quickly got myself decent and opened the door to find...

A dog. A Queensland Heeler mutt. "Boone?"

My dog Boone had been dead for almost fifteen years. I am not ashamed to say I wept.

"How on earth did you get here, boy?" I asked through tears as he tried to lick them away, his whole butt wiggling in the absence of his poor docked tail. I sat there on the floor trying to hold onto him but he kept walking over to the stairs and down. Then coming back up. Each time further down and shorter back. Finally, with just the top of his head peeking back at me I decided to follow him down.

He led me outside. It was dark now. I didn't realize I had been in the shower so long. Unperturbed, Boone pranced into the middle of the parking lot. It looked like most other folks had already gone to bed. "How did you even get inside?" I asked, looking around nervously. Boone just looked up at me with a smug doggy-grin, then without warning he took off running in a circle around me like a centrifuge. At first, I was just confused but he kept running faster and faster, a little grey and black ring around me as a powerful wind kicked up. I had just enough time to register how odd that was when my feet were swept from under me and I found myself tumbling terrified in a cyclone through the sky.

My journey, though traumatic, was short lived. In what seemed like only a few minutes I was placed gently back on my feet where I almost immediately fell down from dizziness, shock, and just good old-fashioned fear of heights. Boone was licking my face as I collected myself on the floor when we were both interrupted by the sound of approaching footsteps. Nervous, I looked at Boone. He didn't look worried so I hoped I didn't need to be either.

The room around me had largely featureless metal walls and the one opposite us held three doorways, each one highlighted curiously in either red, white, or yellow. Through the middle, white-lit doorway, a humanoid figure strode into the room unnaturally pale with a slight shimmer to its skin as they passed under the lights. It was dressed in a smart business casual style with one exception, a somewhat retro-futuristic longsword draped over their left hip. It introduced itself:

"Hello, I don't believe we've met but I've heard much about you. My name is Kit. Sir Kit, to be precise, but there is little use for titles of nobility these days. You must be Ryan Vaughn, you are your father's son."

Now at this point you may be thinking that I am handling this situation very well for a regular person. I must counter both that I was not, at least not in my own feelings, handling it very well, and, I had a little preparation for the more esoteric surprises.

When I was young, my father worked in various places around the world and the family often couldn't go. He would send us stories of how he and The Great Dog Boone would have adventures and save curious characters the world over. Boone would fly down out of the sky in a whirlwind to whisk him off to save the day from gooblies and gobblies or dolliwogs to all manner of evil forces. I always assumed they were BS because my dad is...well we can talk about my dad later. The point being I had heard about some of this stuff so it wasn't the total mindbender it could have been. Nonetheless I was having trouble formulating much in the way of coherent thought.

"Sir...Kit... the guy from the computer? You're real? Boone's real? I mean the tornado and stuff...it was like the Wizard of Oz."

"I have seen that movie, that assessment is accurate. I hope you didn't meet any witches," he stated with a winning smile.

"Is that a thing?"

"Probably, but I have no concrete evidence as yet."

"Wait, was that a joke?"

"Yes, it's something I'm trying more of."

"Oh okay, sorry, I'm just a little startled."

"That is fair."

"How is Boone here?"

"That is both your doing and mine. Come with me."

He began to stride back the way he came, so Boone and I followed, winding our way through a myriad of labyrinthine corridors. Boone pranced ahead, seeming to know the way but still pausing at every object or interruption to investigate. Emerging from an automatic double door that slid open and closed in complete silence, we stood in front of a large bay window looking out over an open room with a device in the center. The device was maybe three stories tall with gaps where blue light shimmered out between the metallic panels. In front of it was a circle of light in the same color, the edges churning into a violent froth of energy.

All around the room emergency lights flashed.

"This is my Imagination Engine." Sir Kit stated with what I could only hear as pride.

"It looks like you're having some difficulties." I responded.

"An astute observation."

"What does this have to do with Boone though?"
"Oh! Boone was the first item to emerge from the engine. I believe that you may have summoned him. The Imagination Engine is sensitive to imaginative impulse and I calibrated it to your familial genetic imprint."

"Are things supposed to come out of it? Wait, my genetic imprint? How did you get that?"

"Hmm, yes, but only when you want. It's not complete yet. I got the idea from watching your father save my people all those years ago. He had such imagination. That was also when I received the genetic material. I managed to collect a small amount from your father and I isolated certain genomic patterns in order to have a reasonable base for the Engine. It should be able to respond to anyone from your bloodline. I was testing this device and Boone emerged first thing. Next thing I knew I could no longer close the gate."

"Wow...That sucks...why am I here?" I looked at Boone. He wagged his butt. "I sent Boone for help, and you are who he brought."

"How am I supposed to help? I don't know anything about this machine. I just saw it for the first time." I responded, incredulous.

"Well, it shouldn't be difficult, I have a good idea what's wrong, I will have Boone fetch the materials while you evacuate the area surrounding the engine of all other new arrivals."
"What?"

"Everything that came through the gate. You have to get it to go back through."

"Me? By myself? Why can't you do it?"

Looking at the floor bashfully, Kit responded, "There are two simple reasons. One, I don't have an imagination. I'm a machine. And secondly, I will need to remain here to launch the purgation sequence."

"How do you mean you don't have an imagination?"

"I designed this as part of a regimen to upgrade myself, this was a proof of concept. Unfortunately, I cannot be completely effective against these beings or in the atmosphere in there. You will have advantages that I do not. I need your help."

"Help? I don't think I can do this. This is ridiculous, I don't even know what's in there! At least my dad was in the Marines, he had training! I couldn't even do laundry until I was 24! There's no way I can do this?"

"You are your father's son."

The repetition of that phrase in the calm, flat voice made me feel ashamed of my outburst. I took three deep breaths.

"What do I need to do?"

"If you can lure all the intruders into the central chamber of the mechanism, I should be able to activate the purgation sequence to return them to their home."

"Should be able to?"

"As of right now the purge sequence is functional. The last functional usage was approximately forty-two minutes ago."

"Well okay, that's pretty recent. I'm not gonna get purged, right?"

"That should not be an issue."

"Should not? Very reassuring."

"The purgation system's effect on carbon-based lifeforms is untested. I have not detected any measurable trace of any known harmful radiations or toxic chemicals."

"Well, I hope I don't get imagination cancer or something..."

"I hope so too."

"Again, very reassuring."

After explaining a few more things we sent Boone away to grab the necessary parts. There was a strong sense of nostalgia watching him bound away over the hills, steadily accelerating into a dark streak across the inscrutable desert terrain outside Kit's facility. Afterwards, Kit helped me suit up into a shiny set of protective coveralls that looked like a Power Rangers costume and I found myself staring at the pressurized hatch that would lead me into the inner sanctum of the machine. Kit's voice sparked up in my ear.

"Oh, I almost forgot. Depending on the strength of the escaping energy fields, you may be able to manifest thoughts corporeally."

"You're saying I can create things with my mind?"

"Potentially yes."

"That seems dangerous."

"Very."

"We really need to work on communicating risks effectively."

The hatch whirred and hissed, slowly opening to reveal the dimly-lit passageway beyond. Fear began to well up inside me as I again began to question my capacity to accomplish this when a statement I had heard on a podcast floated through my mind. "The best remedy for fear is action." I counted to three and I took a single step, then another, and another. By the time I crawled inside the mechanism and closed the hatch behind me, the fear was almost all but forgotten.

I began making my way through the cramped and winding corridors of the outer parts of the machine. I could barely pay attention to where I was actually going because Kit was projecting a map onto the heads-up display of my helmet. I was navigating well enough but the contrast was making it difficult to walk without tripping or running into things. I heard a skittering sound and snapped at Kit to get the map away so I could see what happened.

The map blinked out inside the helmet but now, standing on a shelf level with my face, a spider of about thirteen inches long was raising its spindly legs in a challenge. I leapt backwards and much to my dismay the spider raised on its hind legs and let out a piercing shriek the likes of which I'd only ever heard from little girls or heroines in horror flicks.

"Oh no." I said to no one in particular, but I followed it up with "Kit, where should I be heading?"

"You should be able to make a detour to the left, follow the yellow line I will project on the floor. Be warned: multiple similar contacts detected ahead."

"Why did the spider scream?"

"Unknown."

"It seemed so familiar to me but I can't place it"

Moving forward into the gloom I saw more of these spiders, all at least as large as the first just nesting and pacing and chittering into the gloom. Luckily none seemed to notice me as I crept through the corridors and within short order, I found myself standing at the base of the monolithic structure Kit had shown me and described as the engine's core. It was far more impressive from this angle and I caught myself staring in awe as Kit's voice piped into my head.

"Here is where the energy will be strongest, we should practice corporeal manifestation a few times before we set to work in earnest."

"Whatever you say. Let's give it a shot."

"Very well, I need you to meditate on an object for a moment. It can be anything."

I closed my eyes and tried to settle on something. It turned out to be harder than I thought but eventually I managed to generate a spoon. It flickered into existence in my hand like a bad special effect.

"Excellent" I heard Kit say, "This should make things easier."

With my newfound power I set about thinking of a way to lure things into this room and kicking myself for not doing that before now. I sat trying to recall details of my father's stories and his solutions when Kit spoke over the intercom.

"New interloper incoming."

I turned to face the portal as a sack of bluish membrane slopped out of the portal into a pool of ichor. I watched the membrane distort and snap apart as a hairless doglike thing roughly the size of a German Shepherd ruptured it from inside. A dolliwog, I knew.

"I think you may have inadvertently triggered the portal," chirped Kit.

"I can do that?"

"So, it would seem."

The dolliwog gained its bearings and turned its pale eyes toward me, its slobbering mouth opening to reveal a row of sharp canines. I quickly looked around for some temporary escape, noting only a few protruding sections of bulkhead and some steel support columns. A hideous gurgling cackle sprang from its throat as it launched itself toward me. I made a choice and leapt toward the nearest protrusion in the wall and hauled myself up with a good deal of grunting and said a silent thank you to the man upstairs for the cosmic coincidence that I had recently worked to do my first pull-up in several years.

The beast leapt and snarled around my tenuous sanctuary. It reared up on its hind legs and spat a hideous glob of slime towards my face. I ducked it but it grazed the sleeve of my shirt with a sizzle. Not so safe after all.

"Can you do the purgation sequence now?"

"I can but there's a reset time of one hour and we'd have to wait till then to accomplish the goal."

Not ideal, I thought to myself. What could I do to attract attention? The proverbial lightbulb flashed on in my head just as the dolliwog spat at me again and in my dodge, I misplaced a foot and tumbled off of my high ground. I landed sprawled on the ground, barely managing to protect my head. I sprang to my feet and whirled to find the dolliwog stalking toward me, spittle slick fangs bared. It was close enough now that I wasn't confident I could make another pull-up in time and the fear rose in my gut as I saw the dolliwog tense to spring.

Then, quick as a flash, there was Boone. He drove his body into the monster and they tumbled away snapping and snarling.

"Boone's back?"

"He is very fast, and I think he may have known you were in danger."

Remembering suddenly my goal I sat down and closed my eyes until I felt a weight settle around my shoulders. I opened my eyes to see an electric guitar sitting in my lap, a cable trailing behind me to an amp and a four by twelve speaker cabinet. I don't usually get a chance to play loudly but secret imagination facilities have no neighbors, so I cranked it hard.

I started playing. The sound startled the fighting animals apart and I started advancing on the dolliwog, playing all the while. Boone and I were backing it into a corner when another sound began to rise. Screams. Soft at first but building into a deafening whirlwind of cacophonous sound. Soon the sound of skittering bodies joined it and suddenly from all doors, vents, and crevices poured hundreds upon hundreds of massive shrieking spiders. Boone, having been harrying the dolliwog, instinctively ran to my side as I now scrambled to avoid being overrun by these spiders.

"Activating purge sequence now. Please allow fifteen seconds for the program to boot."

The open doors in the room began a resolute descent as I clambered back onto the raised platform I had occupied. I turned to lift Boone onto the platform when I realized in horror something I hadn't thought of. Boone would likely also vanish in the purge.

"Do I have time to get Boone out?"

"Unlikely."

The thought of it drew unexpected tears to my eyes as I knelt next to Boone. "You have to get out of here Boone Dog, I don't want to lose you again." He looked at me with a quizzical slant to his head. Then he did something that made me feel very stupid. In half a moment I was again caught up in a whirlwind. I caught glimpses of the spiders, the wavering portal, and one very pissed-off dolliwog as I tumbled through the flowing blue light of the imagination engine. I felt a sudden jolt of force in my skull and the world blacked out.

I woke up on a table back in Kit's computer lab with Boone licking at my hand. Kit was typing feverishly with his back turned, but faced me as I sat up.

"Oh good, you're awake."

"What happened?"

"Boone helped you escape but you struck your head against the lowering door as you were carried out. You've been unconscious for three minutes and thirty-three seconds."

That explained the tenderness on the right side of my head.

"Am I okay? I thought you said we wouldn't have time."

"I said that you didn't have time to get Boone out. Vice versa is very different. I did what tests I could and I could not detect any anomalies. I would recommend visiting a medical professional for further analysis."

"Easy enough." I responded. "Did we win?"

"Yes" Kit responded. "I may need more help in the future, however; may Boone and I call on you again?"

I thought for a moment. "Sure" I replied. "I'll try to be more prepared next time." At this, Boone excitedly ran around me once and hopped up to beg for petting. I obliged happily, wondering if imaginary dogs needed to eat. After a few more tests Kit led me back to the room where I had arrived and we said our goodbyes. The whirlwind trip home wasn't nearly as jarring as the outbound one, and when we landed, I didn't even fall down. It was morning by now. I turned and sat next to Boone. Kit and I had agreed it would be best if Boone stayed with him. He wanted to see if Boone could teach him anything about the imagination engine, and my apartment had a no pets policy. I hugged him close to me as he wagged his butt and wiggled around to lick my face.

"You really are a great dog, Boone," I said.

He just sat there panting happily back at me. I patted his head one more time and I headed for the door. He waited till I had the door open and started chasing his tail. I watched the wind pick up as he flew out of sight.

"I'll see you soon. I guess I need to get after some things," I said softly, turning to go inside. "Dolliwogs and screaming spiders, what a day..."

Ryan Vaughn is a writer, musician, and dog-lover based in Bakersfield, California. Ryan works teaching private music lessons and spends his free time writing songs, poetry, and plots for tabletop games. Branching out from his prior output, Ryan Vaughn presents here his first fictional non-fiction story.

Family History

by Kathryn Buys

My family history is a legacy of secrets,

Truths unspoken by us and largely unknown to us.

A false father to replace the true father my
grandmother never knew,

that I fear I may never find.

My family history is bottomless and mysterious as the
sea,

though I know some of it, so much is still hidden from
me,

like a path obscured by early morning fog, like a dark
abyss.

I feel like I do not know my lineage that well.

I found my dad's side and my maternal grandfather's
mother's side,

thanks to documents, but so much of my

family's history is shrouded by the clouds of mystery.

Why are my Dutch-American dad, his siblings, my
cousins, my brother, and I

so much shorter than most Dutch-Americans?

Who was the man on my grandmother's birth
  certificate?

Will I ever know?

Seeking my family lineage is like chasing shadows and
ghosts. The kin I am looking for and those who knew
them well are mostly dust in the earth, gone from my
physical reach. I use whatever resources I can afford as a
lantern, a lantern to bring out the shadows, to break up the
fog separating me and my family from our past.

I walk through the dark cemetery in the early morning
  fog,

a Necropolis of souls long since gone and knowledge
  lost and found.

I shine the lantern across each tombstone,

Hoping, dreaming, praying that the lantern's light will
  show me truth.

Many are still obscure to me, and many I had to
  examine closely to see if there was a connection.

I suppose the best place for me to start is with my
  grandparents,

those that I knew when they were alive,

but about whom I still do not know enough.

I shine my lantern upon the grave of my maternal
grandma. Her side of my family is the side about which I
know the least. I know that her father on her birth
certificate had died when she was not even four years old,

and at her aunt's behest, her mother decided to keep this from her and have the man she remarried be her "father." I know that her mother was German-American, spoke fluent German, and grew up with about four sisters and her father. Both great-grandparents were born in Texas. This is most of what I know about them, and most of my attempts to find pathways to their pasts have led to dead-ends or directions that ultimately seemed false and did not add up with what I knew. My grandma never got to learn about her true father, and did not say much about her mother. I hope the lantern will guide me to her family and allow me to learn more about her past.

My grandma has lived a life of both great joys and great hardships. I could remember my mother telling me about the time she walked to the local bar at the age of ten, where her mother, who drank to cope with chronic pain, and her "father" would be late at night. And standing in the graveyard, dark with fog and clouds, I could imagine what she thought.

I took those steps to the local bar at ten years old.

I knew I would find them there,

I could always find them there.

On a late night,

when my daddy would be tired from a long day,

and when my mother's pain proved too hard to bear,

they knew just how to end the night.

I could always find them there.

But she used that as a lesson. She never wanted her children to experience that, and always made sure she was there for them. And when life brought pain, she and her children could always be there for each other.

On her tombstone in the graveyard, her picture stands beside her name.

> My grandmother was young when this picture was
>   taken.
>
> I gaze into the wide hazel eyes,
>
> which look so much like my own blue ones,
>
> knowing what she would go through.
>
> Finding out the man she called "Daddy" was not her
>   real father,
>
> seeing the man she loved,
>
> that she built her whole life around,
>
> pack his bags and sell the house,
>
> suffering two heart attacks that would leave
>   permanent damage.
>
> And yet, she never lost that gaze.
>
> That graceful, strong gaze.

She had many hardships, but she was strong through them. Eating a peanut butter and jelly sandwich during an earthquake, helping my mom be strong when she was suffering from a brief period of postpartum depression after my brother was born.

Then, I shine my lantern once again upon my paternal grandparents. Unlike my mom's side of my family, I have had little trouble finding documents about my ancestors on my dad's side. Both sets of great-grandparents on my dad's side were Dutch immigrants who traveled to America in the early twentieth century and both of them had well-documented Dutch ancestors who had birth, baptism, marriage, and death records. Sometimes I wonder what happened in the generations leading to my grandparents that led to their problems: my grandfather's sternness and drinking habit during my dad's youth, my grandmother's problems. I may never know. And it seems we often do not know what kind of histories, what blessings and hardships we may inherit from our ancestors. And what makes people who they are, and what makes them do what they do. As I contemplate these ideas, I illuminate my grandparents' tombs and begin to read and dig through the memories and stories I have collected.

My grandma lived a long, good life, with a loving family and a strong faith. She was innocent and godly, bringing up six children and four grandchildren with her husband, my grandpa. But growing up in poverty with a stern, drinking father, it often fell on my dad to take care of my aunts and uncles, as the oldest of the six. Water and biscuits for meals in periods when there was little food and many lean Christmases. My grandpa, from the stories I heard, was stern, having punched my uncle after returning home late from a date, and having driven off my aunts' potential dates in high school. Ironically, he was a doting grandfather to me, my brother, and my cousins. When my brother was in the hospital with a traumatic brain injury after we and our mom were in a car accident, my grandpa came to the hospital in tears, handing my mom a hundred-dollar bill, and telling her to do whatever she could do to save him. When we were children, he would call my female cousin and me *Lieve schatchie*, Dutch for "sweet child" or "darling." Though he was a stern, hard father, he gave my brother and me time and affection that my grandpa on my mom's side did not.

In the cemetery, I take a few steps back near my maternal grandma's tombstone. I shine my light on my maternal grandpa's tombstone, the grandpa whose family I know the most about besides my paternal grandparents' ancestors. His mother was the daughter of Norwegian immigrants who settled in the Midwest as farmers. Her father's family was thoroughly Norwegian; as I could trace them back as far back as the late Middle Ages and early Renaissance. Though the fog still conceals my path to his paternal grandfather's history, I was able to discover some of his grandmother's family. Her paternal grandfather's family was largely Scottish, having immigrated to America in the eighteenth century, with a small number of English and French ancestors. I suspect that my grandfather's maternal family just kept better documents than other many of my other family members. And this was one of the things, besides his work ethic and fun nature, that my mom took pride in about my grandpa.

The second youngest of five, my grandpa served in the Navy during the Korean War. After, he met and married my grandma. For my mom, he was and remains a complicated figure. A doting and fun father for my mom and a strong, hard-working man, my mom looked up to him and saw him as an ideal man.

Then, in the 1980s, after almost twenty-nine years of marriage, my grandpa left my grandma for another woman and sold the family house. My mom's positive perception of her dad, of this ideal man, husband, and dad, was crushed. Because of my grandma's age and emerging health issues, she struggled to find good jobs and eventually had to go on social security. Heartbroken by his betrayal, my grandma depended on my mom to help her. And my grandpa soon stopped paying her alimony like he was supposed to. "I just wasn't happy," he told my mom. My mom could not trust men like she used to. She could not give all of herself like she used to. My uncle dropped out of school. It was in that time that my mom decided that she would never depend on a man so much that she could not live without him. It was in that time that my mom had started to struggle with anger, bitterness, panic attacks, and a buildup of bad habits over the years, that still trouble her over a decade after my grandparents' deaths.

And did my grandpa ever apologize for breaking his family? For breaking my grandma's heart? For breaking both my grandma and my mom's trust? No, of course not. That would have been too easy. Too easy to swallow his pride and admit his guilt instead of projecting it onto my grandma. And though the woman he eventually married was not the woman he left my grandma for, the woman he eventually married was a good, godly woman, it still stung for my mom and my grandma. My mom told me that my grandma just wanted my grandpa to be happy. But happiness at the cost of so much hurt.

And though my grandpa was itching to have grandchildren, was elated when my mom became pregnant with my brother, he soon became far too preoccupied with his second wife's grandchildren. I don't remember him being that attentive towards me, and not as understanding of my autism as my dad's family and my grandma. My step-grandma actually spent more time with me, I remember, than my grandpa did. And when my brother had the brain injury and was in the hospital for two months, my grandpa never visited him, even though he was perfectly able to.

That being said, he still had many good qualities. He was hard-working, hardly ever missed a day of work in the oil fields even when he had a broken wrist. He taught my mom and my uncle to work hard for what they got. He would wake my mom up early to go to the oil rigs with him, which she loved, or to go to Disneyland. Sometimes I look at the picture of my grandfather in his Navy outfit and wonder if he ever thought he would ever be unfaithful to his wife, that he would break his marriage vows, that he would go through several dysfunctional relationships with women before finally meeting and, years later, marrying a woman. Did he love my grandma at any given point? When did he stop? So many questions. Questions that I will probably never know. Questions I will not know until I myself own a tombstone in this cemetery.

I look at the picture of my grandpa in his Navy outfit once again

near his cold, gray tombstone.

His hair is curly and his eyes are small.

In his face and hair, I can see my brother,

and in his eyes, I can see both my brother and my mom.

The same squinty light eyes.

He was a young man then,

striving to work hard and serve his country.

It is hard to reconcile him with the grandpa I grew up with,

or with the deeply flawed man my mom came to discover in her adulthood.

The different sides I know now

remind me how, even in my search for my family history,

pictures and documents only show a small portion of a whole person.

A whole person, obscured and slowly, it seems,

being washed away by the violent, thrashing waves of
time.

That is why stories are so important.

And I will continue to seek these stories,

to find as much truth as I can

even if it takes the rest of my life.

It was learning about my two grandpas that taught me
much of how complicated humans are. That we have good
and bad qualities that do not necessarily single out or
diminish each other. That positive and negative ideas and
possibilities about something can both be true. That good
and evil in many areas is a spectrum of varying actions
and consequences rather than a complete binary of one or
the other. This is a lesson that has stuck with me, that I
need to tell myself continuously. I may continue to travel
the paths through the cemetery and look for the missing
information about my family. But I must remember
perspective, to not idolize the past and put my ancestors
or family line on a pedestal.

While the mysterious fog gives my predecessors

an understandable appeal,

I must remember,

the ancestors I know and the ancestors I seek,

are not necessarily heroes,

not necessarily villains either,

but human, of flesh, bone, and blood.

They are not gods or figures

embodied by the cloud of past virtue and nobility

superior in depth and grandeur than people

here and now, or in the far future.

But with these in mind,

I will continue to search for my past,

to know the truth for myself and for my family.

To see how history has played out in my own family.

Walking through the dark cemetery,

sometimes I feel like the glowing lantern in my hand,

meant to light my way through the fog,

is only making the fog much more pronounced.

As I search for answers to my family's past,

I seem to leave each tombstone with as many
    questions,

if not more.

I don't want to lose the chance to collect the fragments
    of my past

before they disappear once again into the fog and
    winds.

Sometimes I wish I could go through time,

as futile as it is to do so.

As foolish and disastrous as it would likely be.

So I tread the dark, cold cemetery once more,

the lantern the only thing illuminating my path.

Kathryn Buys has a bachelor's degree in English from CSUB and is studying toward her master's degree there. She is also working as a Teacher's Assistant in the CSUB English department and working on her first novel. She lives in Bakersfield, California with her family and her cat Yumi and loves writing, reading, listening to music, walking, pinning story ideas and concepts on Pinterest, researching genealogy, and watching cartoons.

In Noe Valley

by Kevin Shah

When my parents married in 1967, they moved to an apartment in Noe Valley, a neighborhood in San Francisco located in its geographical center. This neighborhood was and is known for being family-oriented. As a family, we lived up to that reputation.

But something was beginning to change that for me.

I spent the earliest days of my life on my mother's lap listening to Bible stories, the Berenstain Bears, and Dr. Seuss. She gave me a love of books during the time I was first learning the power of a mother's love. So, for both of us, books were about bonding.

My memories of her singing are vague but fond. She could read a story and make the characters come alive, all with her voice and her emotions. That was how I first learned about Moses, Elijah, and Jesus.

The kitchen, too, was a place for good food, good stories, and time with my mother.

And this positive relationship with books grew as I learned to read on my own. I eventually learned to read the Encyclopedia Britannica. Our set took up the entire long bookshelf that my parents had assembled from slats of wood and concrete blocks. These giant books taught me everything from ants to the history of Rolls Royce cars to human anatomy, a wonder made more real with colored transparencies.

Our strong bond carried forward because my mother held off going to nursing school until I was five and my sister was seven. Years later she would tell me, "I didn't want someone else to watch my kids." When I did have a babysitter, it was only for a year or so. Her name was Hasta, a gentle, older woman from Sweden with a son named Boo.

I also attended Tiny Tots, a preschool located at Day Park before entering kindergarten at St. Paul's Primary School a few blocks away.

Before I was ten years old, my mother started nursing school, and as a result, I became a "latchkey kid." My sister arrived later than I did, either because she was with friends or had extracurricular activities. So, I usually came home to an empty apartment.

When a child is very young and his mother leaves the room, he and his whole world fall apart. When he is older and his mother leaves, he's okay as long as she quickly returns. A mother's presence makes a house a home. And, if she circles back later in the day with hugs and smiles, then he's okay with longer periods of time without her. Her presence is a promise he hangs onto.

And our house was a home. We were fortunate to have a father who connected with us on every level. For instance, on Sunday evenings, following my weekly bath, my father would pat my hair dry with his large but gentle hands. I had already learned that hands were for loving and holding. Weekday mornings, my father and I would begin our daily walks to my school. And I soon learned that hands were for guiding and defending.

There is no replacement, however, for a mother and her sunshine. Though she may not arrive at home until evening, her presence will warm the child's heart.

Would it have made a difference if she had asked about my day, read books with me, or taken me to the park? It's hard to say. My mother did many things with and for us. Whether it was her fault, my fault, or some combination, we didn't maintain the emotional connection.

One day I had enough. She was asleep during the day, probably following a long shift. I wrote an angry note and slipped it under her door. I don't remember exactly what I wrote, but the basic message was something to the effect of, "Mommy, why don't you spend time with me? You sleep all the time. I hate you!" Years later, my mother would remind me, without bitterness, "Oh yeah, in the letter you said, 'F--- you.'"

After a few minutes, I began to feel terribly, so I quickly wrote a second note and slipped it under the door. "Mommy, I love you, and I'm sorry. Please forgive me." This time she came out. She was groggy but smiling. She hugged me. And I felt a huge weight lift off my shoulders. It was one of the strongest bonding moments with her that I can remember.

She went back to sleep. And I put my concerns to sleep. In time, of course, my concerns would wake up again.

Being home alone as an older child wasn't always bad. I had, of course, expanded the number of books that interested me. There was *The Complete Illustrated Book of Yoga* by Swami Vishnu Devananda. I paid little attention to the reading topics, which included "The Astral Body" and "The Conquest of Death." Instead, I flipped pages, amused by the pictures. Some of the more notable ones featured the swami standing on his head or contorted into a human slingshot while maintain a deadpan facial expression.

Interior design books featured geodesic dome houses, purple wall-to-wall carpeting, houses filled with space-age furniture, and classic houses with carefully coordinated rugs and artwork.

One of my favorite books, *Four Days*, was a tribute to President John F. Kennedy following his assassination. Looking at the pictures of the handsome prince with his wife in her pink pillbox hat and dress reminded me of the charm and class of my parents, as revealed by their wedding pictures.

There was a hidden blessing in being home alone. Once I tired of reading books, I started to write. With my letter to my mother fresh in mind, I wrote my first poems, which were patterned after the Psalms.

I also turned to music, which give me immediate emotional satisfaction. Plugging in my parents' eight-track tapes, I sang along to Judy Collins, Engelbert Humperdinck, and Roger Whitaker. We also owned a turn-table, and I played records from Donna Summer, Funkadelic, Earth, Wind, and Fire, The Bee Gees, and the original Star Wars soundtrack.

There were times I was alone until it got dark. That's when I would often take the music to another level. I took a glass decoration that had a long stem and rounded bottom, something that once flipped upside down, made for a makeshift microphone. Then I climbed on the coffee table and sang to an imaginary arena of screaming fans. I aimed the spotlights on the standing living room lamp on myself. I acted as silly or serious as I wanted, hoping no one would open the front door.

There's only so much music you can listen to, so many books you can read before you get bored again. So, I rummaged through my parents closet and tried on my dad's suit jackets and ties, clomping across the floor with his shoes.

One time, I went to one of my mother's flower pots and ate an ant. The taste was too pungent, too strong, and I quickly spit it out. Another time I was curious about how dirt tasted, so I went to the same flower pot and swallowed a handful of dirt. I threw up out the window.

Then, one day, something happened to force me out of the apartment and begin a new chapter in my latchkey life. I was home alone as usual when something shook. I thought, "Is this my body shaking? Is it the apartment building? Could it be? Could it be?"

The first thing to instill fear in me was not nature, but something my sister had said in the recent past. One day, she stood in the kitchen by the phone with one of her friends. Her voice and face were serious. "Kevin. Do you know that the world is going to end? It's really true." I didn't ask her why, how, or when. I just took that thought to heart. And I knew one thing: she must have heard bad news. At that time, the Cold War was still being waged. But that was only one of the things I feared. Actually, my active little mind looked for clues to the end of the world in everything.

Fear was about to come knocking.

One day, I was sitting on the floor listening to music. Without warning, the apartment shook violently, beginning with the ground. I stood up very quickly. "This is a real earthquake!" I thought. I was seized with an unmistakable urge to run.

Where would I go? Who would I see? The damage was spreading to the rafters, bridges, and foundations of my mind. And being knowledgeable only made it worse – I knew about the San Francisco Earthquake and Fire of 1906, thanks to those darn Encyclopedia Britannica books.

I imagine the that the urge to run during natural disasters is only natural. You want to connect eyes and exchange looks of shock with your neighbors. Then you ask the inevitable question, "Did you feel that?"

Over the next two weeks, there were more shakes.

The "new chapter" official started when I started to explore life outside of the apartment.

At first, my trips were simple and safe. Noe Valley is surrounded by hills which begin two blocks west of our apartment on Duncan. I would visit Bill's Corner Store on the corner of Duncan and Sanchez Streets. There I bought Moritz chocolate Ice Cubes and Coca-Cola in glass bottles. I also discovered and fell in love with 1940s music. Bill and his wife were already in their sixties or seventies, judging by their grey hair. In my adulthood, I went looking for Bill's, but apparently, it had been turned into an apartment or house.

Adventure was now my new companion. I knew about the hills around St. Paul's Primary School, where I had attended. The houses with gabled roofs and bright colors created their own little skyline. Of course, I had plans to explore the "big hill" of Twin Peaks and Diamond Heights, a trendy neighborhood beyond the large hill to the west. Twin Peaks overlooked the most famous part of the San Francisco skyline, the financial district with the TransAmerica Pyramid and Bank of America buildings. But I knew these trips would take time, so I held off.

Postcards and artwork usually will include the Golden Gate Bridge and Coit Tower to round out the San Francisco skyline.

Noe Valley had its own little skyline. St. Paul's Catholic Church had two steeples topped with crosses. And Sutro Tower looked like a ship on stilts. I packed a lunch so I could be prepared for an hour-long hike, wherever that took me. On some of these adventures, I climbed high enough to be able to look back down at my neighborhood. Here, I could see roofs, east towards Potrero Hill, and to St. Paul's piercing towers. Houses now looked more like Monopoly game pieces.

So ironic that I was now becoming acquainted with the neighborhood known for its affinity for families while at the same time becoming a stranger to my family. At least for the better part of each afternoon. I had gotten a taste of adventure and wanted more.

On one of my more ambitious hikes, I climbed the last street before a series of steps that rose on either side of a miniature hill and a low-hanging block wall that led to Noe Street. From there, I could walk to another miniature hill. And that was a landmark, because as I understood it, that was the western end of Noe Valley – the final frontier. I decided I would hike no further. And while indoors I might have read books, outdoors, I read my neighborhood. Even though this was almost ten years before the devastating Loma Prieta Earthquake of 1989, San Franciscans were expecting the "Big One." The hills I climbed had small- and medium-sized cracks. Cracks that I read the same way a palm reader reads folds and lines in the skin of a person's palm. What did the future hold for my city?

San Francisco will not let you worry about earthquakes too long before she presents you with new fascinations and a handful of things that shake your senses. I hadn't yet been to the Castro District, a gay neighborhood only a few blocks away. But one day I visited a friend's house and wandered into a room where, to my shock, I saw his mother lying under the covers with another woman.

I would often enter the basement of an apartment building across the street from ours. One day, I found Alejandro, a schoolmate's older brother sniffing spray paint out of a plastic bag. His head was dipped back as though he was taking in life-saving oxygen. I had watched in shock as a policeman had thrown him through a store-front window – an act that I saw as angry and hateful.

Another time, I saw a van turned on its side. Then there were the school kids on Church Street who rode the backsides of light rail vehicles, standing on the junctions designed to join cars. Seeing these wild things was like rapidly turning channels on late night television.

If I had paid attention to the growing wiliness, I might have sensed that the neighborhood cats were creeped out by everything I saw. As they negotiated the undersides of cars and the corners of buildings, they might have meowed the words, "Kevin, go home."

And looking back, this was all the familiar beginning of a typical downward spiral. One day, I climbed the roof of our apartment building. Before long, I was freely walking the roofs of the adjacent apartment buildings and houses. There was no specific destination I had in mind; I just climbed because I could. I was like a miniature James Bond without a cause. Below me, people walked the neighborhood. Cars drove up and down the street. I could see many of Noe Valley's Victorians, a kind of house San Francisco is known for.

Then there was the alley one block over where I entered an unlocked garage on a regular basis just to hang out. The interior was old and wooden, and old tools hung on the walls. I never touched anything, just marveled at this strange world away from home. There was also what was either an abandoned car or one whose owner didn't care about visitors or car jackers. Here I banged on the seats like they were tom-toms, pretending to out-drum Mark, whose band performed the Beatles' "Day Tripper" for a talent show at school.

Adults sometimes ask their kids, "Why did you do that?" The reply, if the kid is honest is, "Why not?" As if to illustrate that point, one day, after school, I left one of the auditorium doors ajar. I quietly went home and waited an hour. At the appointment time, I quietly walked back to the school, and looking around to make sure was alone. I quietly opened the door and slipped into the auditorium. This was the same place we went each year as a family for the school carnival. We would pitch dimes or play Bingo.

Being alone in the darkened auditorium, my footsteps echoed against the walls. I opened every door to every room so I could enter in. No goal to steal or vandalize. But I did wonder if those carnival dimes might still be in the auditorium. The excitement followed me into every room until, out of the corner of my eye, I could see the light pouring in through cracks in the door casing. Maybe it was a symbol of the light of conscience that now entered my darkened mind.

My ultimate adventure was to climb the tallest of the two steeples of the church. I knew there was a passage that probably began at the balcony of the church auditorium. St. Paul's church was completed in 1911. According to legend, a man who was painting the steeples fell to his death in front of the church. There was a stone circle built in the supposed spot where he landed. I had no way up, because the church is separate from the school.

I had to ask myself if all this exploring meant that I was really free. In the first place, I had done nothing to overcome my fear of earthquakes, so I wasn't off to a great start.

Bonding was another reality that we would have to grapple with as a family for years to come. That whole crisis was in its early stages and would follow me into my twenties.

There was a deeper fear I was beginning to face: my own depravity. I could escape the apartment if I was bored and find adventure. But I had to face the fact that I was far from innocent. Sometimes I entered the neighboring apartment building foyer before the electric security door could close. Sometimes I entered the neighboring garage to gawk at the biggest car in the world, a brown Lincoln Town Car.

I just couldn't escape myself and what I was becoming. And before I was eight years old, I entered a neighbor's apartment and stole several Matchbox cars. The good thing was that I felt ashamed and guilty. And I broke down in tears while confessing to my surprised but grateful parents. And, for the most part I stopped stealing things at that time.

There are also the questions I should have asked but didn't, perhaps because I was too young and busy exploring.

For instance, why didn't I call my dad at work each day to say hello? Why didn't I tell my mother exactly what I needed? Perhaps I felt it would make no difference if I did.

Looking back, I can understand that my parents had bigger plans: several years later, they bought a house by the ocean. Pacifica was a coastal and hilly city of 30,000 that would prove friendlier than San Francisco. A city in which, for the first time in my life, complete strangers would say hello to me.

Instead of wandering Noe Valley, I could have gone to my grandmother's house. We called her Mamita, which means "little mommy" in Spanish. She lived on Cesar Chavez Street, known then as Army Street. That was only three blocks away. There, I could have spent time with her, my cousin, and my aunt. They were always cooking Salvadorian food and fish, which I saw as a delicacy. My grandmother's apartment was, at times, a home away from home. When I spent the night, my cousin Jacqueline and I watched black and white movies and sang to Elvis records.

At Mamata's, on a ledge at the back of the kitchen, there was a fish tank. My cousin and I took turns feeding my grandmother's giant goldfish. I could have stared in awe as the goldfish swam circles and came up to the glass.

I could have, but I didn't.

What was I becoming? Too busy to ask for help? Too scared to admit that I was scared for no apparent reason?

I had watched Mamita hold out her arms to her goldfish, and, with much feeling declare, "These are my grandsons!! My GRANDSONS!!" with so much sincerity I thought she would cry.

Had I showed up and told her how I felt, what I needed, and who I needed, she could have cried for me, opened her arms. She could have called out, "Keving, you are my grandson, my GRANDSON!" and held me close to her heart.

At age fifty, I drove north from my new home in Bakersfield to visit my parents in the Bay Area. Before spending time with my mother, I hiked up to a San Francisco landmark for the first time in my life. The Cross of Mt. Davidson stands one hundred and three feet tall. It rises only blocks above the house where my parents lived briefly before moving to Noe Valley. The Cross had been tiny in my life then. Now it stood tall and strong.

The Cross is no mere symbol of redemption, but a historical reality that brought me spiritual adoption and forgiveness. And because of this most valuable piece of the skyline, I could make a new commitment. I could tell my mother what I needed from her, but that was not so important for me. Now I could focus on giving her what she needed then and now – the love of her son.

Kevin Shah is a native of San Francisco and a longtime Bakersfield resident. He has two grown kids, teaches high school, and has published poetry, literary humor, and scholarly research. He has been featured twice on Valley Public Radio's Valley Writers Read. Currently he is working on a family-inspired novel.

Unsung Heroes – Honoring those Millions

by Scott Brown

Rockford, Illinois – On a cool Fall Saturday afternnon
in the Midwest

Dad was driving us down from our hometown of Rockford, Illinois to Chicago on a Saturday afternoon to see some special displays he said would help us understand how World War II came to an end.

Rockford was just as ordinary a town as any other hundred U.S. towns that popped up in the great expansion to the west, except for us Browns it is where my great-great-grandfather settled in the 1800s, opening a small mercantile store, which by the 1940s had become a half-square block two-story department store.

Rockford is where my dad worked during the war in a manufacturing plant making little, ordinary metal and rubber hose clamps for essential cooling systems in thousands upon thousands of war planes and trucks. Dad told us he was a pacifist and that job kept him out of the battles of war.

My family had just celebrated my sixth birthday the day before, and I was in the back seat as usual with my kid brother. We were setting up my birthday gifts, making a miniature campground with tents, picnic tables and fireplaces on the seat between us. We were good at finding things to do, especially if it helped us stay out of trouble on a two-hour road trip.

Dad told us the wide sweeping war had three different dates for the last day when the enemy surrendered due to the spread-out geography between the Allies. The official European/American date was May 8, 1945. Today was August 29, 1945. Most parts of the world had begun to recover from the anxiety of day-after-day bombing and horrors of war.

The City of Chicago decided to commemorate the end of the five-year war by displaying German uniforms, guns, sabers, and other wartime paraphernalia as a sign of defeat of the Furor and his colossal war machine.

These were fascinating moments, and some not so, that shaped our lives in the aftermath of a very disarrayed world.

As afternoon turned to evening the streets of Chicago became brightly lit. We stood on the outside looking in at what was seemingly meant to be picture windows in row after row of department stores and office buildings set side-by-side down long city blocks with many war reminders glaring back out at us.

The intensity of RED and BLACK and CHROME colors shining off the collections of German troops clothing and instruments of war were now souvenirs stripped off the fallen German soldiers, generals, commanders, and out of tank battalions and downed airplanes. It was overwhelming to each of us Browns in whatever different ways we could consume it.

Our 'American safe-at-home-senses' didn't really know what to make of all this captured evidence of a completely broken Nazi Regime. At six years of age I had no idea of the extent of unsung heroes who had fought for our liberty and gave of their lives on the battlefields. Dad told us as we all stood there in awe that FDR, our President Roosevelt, had helped bring an end to WWII.

Now in 2021 with seventy-six years gone by and the Covid-19 Pandemic refusing to die, a new United States President had taken office. He was reminded of the post-WWII days of his predecessor, FDR, who readily administered the return to normal.

The new President had been troubled by the pandemic's huge numbers of EMT and health provider heroes, the family heroes who stuck by the healthcare windows looking in at their relatives dying, and the plight of the funeral director heroes attempting to accommodate the mounting numbers of dead and all their families, to mention just a few.

Early in his new administration the President, in a time of difficult concern, decided to honor all those Covid-19 unsung heroes and the lives of their departed family members.

Friday Afternoon Before the Unsung Hero Presentation

The President and First Lady had come to enjoy hot coffee and sweet cakes in the late summer on Friday afternoons after a busy presidential week. The Secret Service had cleared the usual balcony on the west side of the White House and housekeeping arranged the same selected table and two chairs for the POTUS and his bride. This was their third date.

As they settled in this popular spot away from the maddening crowd, the First lady spoke, "Dearest, the front desk tells me you are scheduled to deliver an award this weekend. Please tell me about it."

"Yes, Kitty. As I had mentioned, I decided to acknowledge the Unsung Heroes that we have an abundance of here in America. They don't get the press they deserve and surely not often enough."

"Mr. President dear, I have a question."

"Of course. What is that Kitty?"

"Are these Unsung Heroes generally known or unknown and have to be found?"

"For the most part they are unknown, dear one. And how we find them is a story in and of itself.

"This evening I'll tell you the start of the story how my scouts found the young girl who is first up, and then next time we rendezvous, I'll give you the rules for finding the next unsung hero."

He pauses and looked up at his wife adding, "Okay?"

She in turn set down her cup and placed her hand on top of his replying, "Okay with me Chief. I love your story-telling. You are a great teller. I can hardly wait."

"Thank you, Kitty, you are kind to say that. Here is a prelude to Miss Jao Patel.

"Jao is 15 and is already a junior in high school. She is first generation East Indian, being the second child of Mr. and Mrs. Hapgu Patel, who immigrated to the U.S. in 2005 from Bombay, India. They settled in Highland, New Jersey, where Mr. Patel had been recruited to head up the new Zenith Health Ventures vaccine plant.

"Jao was born the year after they arrived in the U.S. She was home schooled through 7th grade at which time testing showed at thirteen years old she could enter 9th grade for her first year of high school."

"That is remarkable dear just in itself, let alone what she did to earn this Unsung Hero honor?"

"You are right. Glad you asked Kitty; however we must leave shortly for the State Dinner.

"Jao had been excited with the advancements in medicine in America and the vaccinations she had received here. So she asked her parents for a chemistry set for her 11th birthday and a tour of the Zenith Health Ventures Advanced Medicine Research Department where her dad works.

"Three months later, she told her Dad she had understood the development phase of new vaccines and wanted to offer her solution to the Covid-2021 Delta Variant Virus. Her dad was quite amazed and told his chief researcher who in turn invited Mr. Patel and Jao to tour the lab. The rest is what they say is history.

"At the end of the tour Jao, being very impressed, politely spoke to the chief and her dad that she knew she had found the chemical additive to conquer Covid-2021.

"The chief agreed to review her finds and, doing so, the vaccine was developed, tested, and worked as expected. It is now being made and soon to be distributed. When her mother heard this, Mrs. Patel told friends who told friends who told our Vice President. And tomorrow our young Unsung Hero will meet the United States public at the Lincoln Memorial with 5,000 locals invited.

"And at that time my dear Kitty, you will hear the rest of the story. Okay?"

"Astonishing Chief. Yes, okay. Let's go to dinner."

The Next Day - Saturday afternoon at the Lincoln Memorial

The gathering of admirers had swelled larger than expected. The clouds had parted, the sun blessed the event with summer warmth, and the grandstands were quickly filling to capacity.

The President's Envoy approached the podium, raised the microphone tapping it twice. It echoed back. He straightened and spoke, "Good afternoon. This is a very special day. We are here today to praise people we don't know and haven't met before."

The crowd hushed, turning to each other, with someone asking, "What did he say?" Another said, "I thought we came to honor people of great stature."

The speaker raised his voice. "My dear friends, listen closely. This is truly a very important day. Our President has designated today in in memory of America's Unsung Heroes."

Again the crowd let out a low rumble of grumbling of not understanding, of not expecting, of questioning what they just heard.

A loud voice boomed back startling the crowd. Everyone again looked straight ahead, and smiles came over their faces.

President Van Hoover had moved into place at the podium and was excitingly waving to the audience. He was beaming, ready to introduce the first Unsung Hero.

"Dear friends, I am so pleased and grateful we can come together like this to honor America's Unsung Heroes.

"I ask you, 'Do each of you know an Unsung Hero?'"

"Do you know why we address people we don't even know as Unsung Heroes?" He paused with a smile.

"Would you all like to meet an Unsung Hero?"

People looked around at each other, all perhaps wondering if the person next to them was indeed an unsung hero.

One middle-aged lady spoke up, "I never thought about the idea of someone I don't even know could be a hero."

The man next to her responded, "You mean like my neighbor Jim who got up every morning for 30 years to deliver newspapers from 5 to 7 a.m.? I came to just expect my paper and coffee to be there never giving him the credit!"

The President beamed witnessing the exchange in the crowd caught up in this new thinking of Unsung Heroes.

At the right moment he spoke up, "Again friends and people out across America, here is how this all came about."

The President was about to make another startling announcement that he wanted to tell all of us in the crowd.

He continued, "I asked my staff to compile a list of names of people they could identify as Unsung Heroes in America. I advised them of the two elements that were a requirement. One was the fact that the candidates must exhibit 'Obscurity'."

"Obscurity to me means we may have never known these unsung heroes but we would love to learn who they are.

"And two, that the action of heroism may have taken place outside our country, yet it was for the betterment of our country and the world."

The President again listened to the murmuring and growing excitement coming from the audience. He continued:

"It is now my extreme pleasure to introduce our first selected American Unsung Hero."

As the President turned to his right, a young lady stepped forward out of the shadows behind the podium. The President took her hand, bringing her up front for the crowd to see her.

"Ladies and gentlemen please meet and welcome Miss Jao Patel, our very first Unsung Hero. I know you will all be amazed at what she has done for the betterment of society."

The audience rose and stood together as Jao waved to the crowd who seemed to be warming to the idea of the unknown Unsung Hero. Many waved back.

The President and Jao moved around the podium and he continued her introduction.

"I have asked Jao Patel to come join us here today, as she is truly an Unsung Hero."

The young girl awkwardly smiles and stepped a little closer to her new friend. "Jao is a true example of someone dedicated to a cause and yet is a quiet, hardworking 15-year-old junior in high school.

The President pauses and the crowd whispers admiration as some begin to clap.

"And do you have any idea what she does in her spare time after school and homework?"

With no response, the audience awaits the answer.

"She invents things. She invents things that save people's lives, that enhance people's lives."

He hesitates once again.

"Do you want to know the latest thing Jao invented?"

The crowd answered in unison, "Yes!"

The President turns toward Jao as the clapping increases.

He leans into the microphone and raising his voice he proclaims, "The Covid-2021 Variant Vaccine."

The folks, all 5,000, let out a low gasp, again turning to each other. Someone asks, "Can you believe what he just said?"

The President had put his arm around Joa's shoulders, giving her a hug. She felt the comfort of a believer and smiled much bigger.

"Yes I said, 'she invented the Covid-2021 Delta Variant Vaccine.' which Franklin Pharmaceuticals in Des Moines, Iowa is going to manufacture.

"Her contribution will bring garner a reward of satisfaction for her and her family, a fully-paid scholarship to Stanford University, and the knowing she contributed to saving millions of people's lives."

The crowd still standing, erupted in applause as they celebrated the young Unsung Hero. Their clapping went on for minutes.

The President finally raises his arms and speaks loudly into the mic, "And how did she do this? With a high-school-level chemistry set that her mother and father bought for her twelfth birthday, along with her never-wavering sense she had found the missing link to enhance the vaccine.

"Her father, a highly esteemed chemist, was her mentor and cheerleader. Jao worked after school day after day to find the necessary chain of elements that would contribute to the workability of this next vaccine carrier."

The President asked for silence and then raised up a large bright red envelope, opening it to remove a beautifully framed object.

He spoke, "And this is evidence for Jao that she has earned our first Unsung Hero Award Certificate Number 0001 for her accomplishments done behind the scenes of her normal daily walk. She put to use her interests, her beliefs, and the spare time we all choose to use in some fashion or another after our usual daily activities are done."

He handed the prize certificate to Jao. She hugged it close to her heart. It was far more that she had ever anticipated.

She waved to us and to her family sitting in the front row setting her hand over her heart with a big smile.

After Chicago and all the unsung heroes of WWII we could only imagine, I would not have missed this upbeat event on a bet.

The Envoy, waiting in the background off to the side, knew 9,999 other awards were planned over the President's term and yet to be made, many in fact, yet to be found.

He gave the President credit for what this extraordinary day meant to the crowd, which along with Kitty, now knew the backstory of the true story of our Unsung Heroes, those who are known and those who are yet to be found and named.

Kitty, witnessing the ceremony while standing off from the podium, smiles and whispers under her breath, "That's my chief." She took a deep breath of evening air.

And with great admiration, she utters, "Love that man. He has such a big heart for unsung heroes."

Scott Brown is a native of snowy Illinois. His family, searching for sunny days, headed to California in 1946. Scott has lived on or near the beach ever since. Bakersfield beckoned in 1982 with large oil field development seeking his knowledge (beach –1½ hours). He became smitten with writing and publishing after eons of engineering dream projects. He has lots of children as subjects and loves travel to research and write inspirational fiction stories, novels and educational books. His passion is inventing new style books – ask him!